PRESENTED TO

_____

DATE

_____

BY

_____

OCCASION

_____

The Best Things Ever Said about Parenting

Other books by the Carmichaels

Lord, Bless My Child

The Best Things Ever Said about Parenting

Compiled by **BILL & NANCIE CARMICHAEL**

Tyndale House Publishers, Inc.
WHEATON, ILLINOIS

Library of Congress Cataloging-in-Publication Data

Carmichael, William, date
  The best things ever said about parenting / compiled by Bill and Nancie Carmichael.
    p.   cm.
  ISBN 0-8423-0151-8
  1. Parenting—Religious aspects—Christianity.   2. Family—Religious life.
  I. Carmichael, Nancie. II. Title.
BV4526.2.C267 1996
248.8'45—dc20   96-17772

Printed in the United States of America

01 00 99 98 97 96
 7   6   5   4   3   2   1

We dedicate this book
to the millions of parents
who are in the trenches,
giving everything they have
to raise good kids.

ACKNOWLEDGMENTS

Thanks to Ruthie Keller, Jan Johnson, and Nancy Kennedy for their help in finding many of the quotations included in this book.

Thanks to Lynn Vanderzalm for her editorial leadership in seeing this book to its completion and to the wonderful Tyndale staff, whose creativity and expertise are beyond compare.

Thanks also to the many people whose thoughts and insights are captured in the quotations in the following pages. Their gems of wisdom equip all of us pilgrims to become better parents.

"Pretty Good Parents"

From the day our first child was born, we knew we needed all the help we could get. When I was fresh out of graduate school with a degree in educational counseling (and before our first child was born), I was ripe with expert advice for my older sister, who had two young daughters. I observed her anxiety, self-doubt, and frustration and could not understand what all the fuss was about. I gave her fresh insights and hot tips that I knew would solve all of her parenting problems. In my mind, raising children was a piece of cake. You just follow a few simple formulas, and bingo . . . success!

By the time our second son had arrived and I had exhausted all of my learned theories, I was the one asking for advice from seasoned veterans. Nancie and I suffered the same anxieties and misgivings that other parents suffered. These unique little creatures who came into our homes and hearts became the most challenging vocation of our lives.

As parents of five children, Nancie and I gave up trying to be perfect parents long ago. We realized that the idea of a parenting "expert" is only an idea. After reading Lewis Smedes' book *A Pretty Good Person,* we decided that our goal is just to be "pretty good parents."

Over the years of rubbing shoulders with some other pretty good parents, writing and editing articles for the parenting magazine we founded, and reading most of the books written about parenting, we have collected what we consider to be some of the best wisdom about parenting.

We have in our files literally thousands of quotations that have inspired us, that have caused us to stop and ponder, or that have given some advice that was easy to remember. This book includes time-honored wisdom from men, women, and children who have made some profound statements about families, parents, and home.

In the twenty-seven years Nancie and I have been involved in ministry to families and in parenting our own children, we have discovered that our most important role as parents is creating a healthy home for our children. What makes a home healthy? We have settled on seven foundational principles that we believe make a home a safe and nurturing environment in which children can grow.

A healthy home is

> A place of *Purpose*
> A place of *Formation*
> A place of *Celebration*
> A place with *Boundaries*
> A place of *Refuge*
> A place of *Connection*
> A place with a *Legacy*

We hope that these quotations will mean as much to you and your family as they have meant to us. One bit of advice. Ponder the sayings in this book. On first blush, some will seem to have an obvious meaning—or no deep meaning at all. But slow down. Think about the words. Let the words sink in. They will give you great insight. And they may even help you become a pretty good parent.

Bill Carmichael

Part
One
Purpose

Home is where I learn about the deeper meaning of life: spirituality, purpose, the "why" of life. I learn Bible verses, doctrine, catechism. I learn about God, about grace and forgiveness. I form my thinking about death and what happens after death. I learn that I am more than body and mind; I am also spirit. I learn faith and how to let my spirit soar into God's Spirit. I experience what spiritual devotion is.

Home is where concepts like spirit, heaven, eternity, God, sin, confession, forgiveness, grace, love, redemption, worship, humility, and sacrifice all take on meaning. Home is where my first stumbling, childlike prayers are heard. It is where the Bible is read, believed, and put into practice.

Home is where I learn that God is in charge and that life has order. I realize that having rules, laws, and constraint benefits both the whole of society and me personally. I learn that I am protected by being accountable. I understand that with freedom comes responsibility.

Home is a place with a purpose. It is where a life mission is lived out, where a larger-than-us perspective of life prevails, a place with eternity in mind. It is a place that looks at how we can be part of God's plan for his kingdom.

My home's "purpose" determines where our family lives, how we spend our money and our spare time. Our family purpose sets our values and our priorities.

The quality of our family life, as well as our relationships with each other, our extended family, and our fellow human beings are all directly related to our family's *purpose*.

In short, home gives me a set of beliefs that are foundational to the way I view the world. These beliefs are the glass through which I look to view life, the filter by which I process all information, the formula for how I make choices and decisions.

The real parents of our children
are the ideas that govern us.

Polly Berrien Berends
Gently Lead

We're so consumed with the feeding, the dressing, the buckling into car seats, the finding of bathrooms, and the counting of heads that we sometimes forget that there is any greater mission to raising children than making sure the crusts are cut off the sandwiches and that everybody gets a balloon.

Joyce Maynard
"Hopes and Prayers," *Parenting* magazine

You, as a mother or father, are charged with the responsibility of training up your children in the way they should go. That may be the most important task you will be given in your lifetime. No other accomplishments and no other success will compensate for failure to teach these eternal truths to the generation now around your knees.

**Gloria Gaither and
Shirley Dobson**

Let's Hide the Word

nfortunately, many families today don't stand for anything. Neither "little churches" nor "little commonwealths," they are more like "little hotels"—places where one stays temporarily but with no particular sense of commitment.

William Kilpatrick
Why Johnny Can't Tell Right from Wrong

Somewhere . . . there is the child who will paint the greatest picture or carve the greatest statue of the age; who will deliver his country in an hour of peril; give his life for a great principle; another born more of the spirit than of the flesh who will live continually on the heights of moral being and in dying will draw others to morality. It may be that I shall preserve one of these children to the race. It is a peg big enough on which to hang a hope. For every child is a new incarnate thought of God, an ever fresh and radiant possibility.

Kate Douglas Wiggin

Virtue magazine

The greatest use of life is to spend it for something that will outlast it.

William James

ommitment is the invisible fiber that binds a collection of individuals into a caring community. A large one or a small one. Everything depends on it. Everything from a family reunion to a concord of nations, from calling a committee meeting to founding a nation, from celebrating high mass to getting a return trip ticket to Pasadena. Not to mention a lasting marriage. Or a good friendship. Maybe you can have a regime, or a gang, or a crowd, or a prison full of inmates, or even a foreign legion, without commitment, but you cannot have a human community.

Lewis Smedes
Caring and Commitment

You made all the delicate, inner parts of my body and knit me together in my mother's womb. Thank you for making me so wonderfully complex! Your workmanship is marvelous—and how well I know it.

THE BIBLE
Psalm 139:13-14

used to think how wonderful it would be to have perfect children. Now I know how much they would miss by being too good. I don't want perfect children: I want something far better for them than that! I want them to know the power of the Holy Spirit, to feel God's hand of change in their lives, and to recognize the depth of their need for the blood of Jesus Christ. I want them to know the power of renewal.

Karen Scalf Linamen

The Parent Warrior

All that is not eternal is eternally out of date.

C. S. Lewis
The Four Loves

The world is moved along, not only by the mighty shoves of its heroes, but also by the aggregate of the tiny pushes of each honest worker.

Helen Keller

When NASA launched the first space shuttle, you can bet that they didn't tell the crew, "Let's just fly around for a while and see if we find anything interesting." While this sounds ridiculous, it's exactly what many parents do every day by not having a clear purpose for being.

William Carmichael

What our deepest self craves is not more enjoyment but some supreme purpose that will give unity and direction to our life. We can never know the profoundest joy without a conviction that our life is significant—not a meaningless episode.

Kenny J. Goldring

as quoted in *The Gift of Family*
by Naomi Rhode

The reason why the rise of psychology has not ushered in the reign of happiness is that although it provides skills for life, psychology has never been able to say anything about the purpose of life. . . . Psychology books have no plot.

William Kilpatrick
Why Johnny Can't Tell Right from Wrong

So, awed by the beauty and goodness of our children, dumbfounded by our failure to be the parents we hoped to be, worshiping, giving horsey rides, and picking up peas, we are brought to our knees. It is a good idea to learn to pray. As the atom is smashed to release tremendous physical energy, so through prayer we smash the limits of personal power for good and ill.

Polly Berrien Berends

Gently Lead

Naturally, prayer is not practical, it is absurd; we have to realize that prayer is stupid from the ordinary common-sense point of view.

Oswald Chambers
My Utmost for His Highest

Prayer is the mortar that holds our house together.

Mother Teresa

Give your children up to God. It is utterly safe to place your children in God's sure hands.

John White
psychologist and author

In an era when many parents are protesting against laws that prohibit prayer in school, it would be revealing to survey those very parents to find out how much praying goes on at home.

Anonymous

believe I need to pray for my children: for their salvation, for their protection, for the development of their characters.

But I also need to pray for the people who influence them daily: their teachers, their peers, their closest friends, and me.

Karen Scalf Linamen
The Parent Warrior

The fact that "charity begins at home" does not mean it should end there. Children can help with community drives, with environmental cleanups, with collecting money for worthy causes, with church work. However, the most important experiences are person to person: visiting a sick relative, helping elderly neighbors with chores, delivering groceries to a shut-in, baby-sitting without charge for a family experiencing an emergency.

William Kilpatrick
Why Johnny Can't Tell Right from Wrong

Prayer is exhaling the spirit
of man and inhaling the Spirit
of God.

Edwin Keith

as quoted in *A Man's Work Is Never Done*
by David Z. Nowell

Give your troubles to God; He will be up all night anyway.

Unknown

O Christ, do not give me tasks equal to my powers, but give me powers equal to my tasks, for I want to be stretched by things too great for me. I want to grow through the greatness of my tasks, but I shall need your help for the growing.

E. Stanley Jones

Prayer is a shield to the soul, a sacrifice to God, and a scourge to Satan.

John Bunyan

Maybe we should take a tip from the sparrow in the psalm. She built her nest in a place near God's altar. She lived where God lived. We parents who want to spend time with God can do so when we build a nest near him and then spend everyday moments in it with him.

Elisa Morgan
"Nesting Instinct,"
Christian Parenting Today magazine

And now a word to you fathers. Don't make your children angry by the way you treat them. Rather, bring them up with the discipline and instruction approved by the Lord.

THE BIBLE
Ephesians 6:4

To some this world may seem like no place to bring up a child. And in some respects they are right. But we take that risk anyway with the comforting knowledge that it is not for this world that we prepare them.

Karen L. Tornberg
Family Traditions That Last a Lifetime
by Karen M. Ball and Karen L. Tornberg

Those who trust in the Lord
are as secure as Mount Zion;
they will not be defeated
but will endure forever.

THE BIBLE
Psalm 125:1

Nobody ever outgrows
Scripture; the book widens
and deepens with our years.

Charles H. Spurgeon

have held many things in my hands and have lost them all; but that which I have committed to God, that I still possess.

Martin Luther

The desperate need today is not for a greater number of intelligent people, or gifted people, but for deep people.

Richard Foster

Celebration of Discipline

Parents who never read God's Word outside of an organized meeting of the church are not likely to sense the urgency of instructing children in the most important truth in the world. If we really believe that knowing God and His Son is the most vital experience in the world, how dare we leave the responsibility for instruction to someone else?

Gladys Hunt

Honey from the Rock

Some children were brought to Jesus so he could lay his hands on them and pray for them. . . . Jesus said, "Let the children come to me. Don't stop them! For the Kingdom of Heaven belongs to such as these." And he placed his hands on their heads and blessed them before he left.

THE BIBLE
Matthew 19:13-15

Purpose in life is not to find your freedom, but your Master.

G. Campbell Morgan
as quoted in *Go for the Magic* by Pat Williams

Spiritual battles need to be fought with spiritual weapons.

Greg Johnson and Mike Yorkey

Faithful Parents, Faithful Kids

God does not have any grandchildren, only children.

David Du Plessis

When home is ruled according to God's Word, angels might be asked to stay with us, and they would not find themselves out of their element.

Charles H. Spurgeon

The best way for a child to learn to fear God is to know a real Christian. The best way for a child to learn to pray is to live with a father and mother who know a life of friendship with God.

Johann Heinrich Pestalozzi

Part
Two
Formation

Home is where I learn life's virtues. Home is where I learn love, character, commitment, work, and self-discipline. Home gives lessons in doing chores, working as a team, giving in, negotiating, treating others well, sharing, telling the truth, and caring. Home is the place that teaches me how to cope with adversity, pain, persecution, injustice, and even death. It teaches me about sex, finances, cleanliness, and manners.

At home I learn how to work, ride a bike, mow a lawn, play a musical instrument, change the oil in my car, fix a meal, wash my clothes, make my bed, sweep the floor, and earn money.

Home demonstrates the value of reading a book, keeping a journal, telling a story, and singing a song.

In my home I form my view of life—what to embrace, what to abhor, what to feed my mind, and how to think.

In short, home forms my character for life.

Babies are such a nice way
to start people.

Unknown

Most of us prefer bright, calm, storm-free days—days filled with serenity. The Lord has promised not to give us more trouble than we can take. In his presence, he offers to each of us enough serenity to keep us going one day at a time. With him we can be bright and steady no matter what the family barometer reads.

Gigi Graham Tchividjian

Christian Parenting Today magazine

hate to see my children suffer, but loving them means doing what is best for them, not what hurts the least.

Patti Covert
Family Life

t's important to let our kids know we are aware of our inadequacies. Tell them. You have nothing to lose in honestly admitting to them that you didn't do everything correctly as a parent. That admission may be the key to opening communication and beginning the process of healing your relationships with your kids.

**Stephen Arterburn
and Jim Burns**

When Love Is Not Enough

Where will our country find leaders with integrity, courage, strength—all the family values—in ten, twenty, or thirty years? The answer is that you are teaching them, loving them, and raising them right now.

Barbara Bush

as quoted in *Family Traditions That Last a Lifetime*
by Karen M. Ball and Karen L. Tornberg

Why should we fuss over a guest at the door but fail to acknowledge when a loved one enters? Every home needs at least one person [who] is custodian of the welcome!

Mimi Wilson and Mary Beth Lagerborg

Table Talk

Hospitality is the way we turn
a prejudiced world around,
one heart at a time.

Joan D. Chittister
Wisdom Distilled from the Daily

Small boys learn to be large men in the presence of large men who care about small boys.

Phyllis Theroux
Night Lights

When Thomas Edison was working on improving his first electric light bulb, the story goes, he handed the finished bulb to a young helper, who nervously carried it upstairs, step by step. At the last possible moment, the boy dropped it—requiring the whole team to work another twenty-four hours to make a second bulb. When it was finished, Edison looked around, then handed it to the same boy. The gesture probably changed the boy's life. Edison knew that more than a bulb was at stake.

James D. Newton

The Great American Bathroom Book III

Words such as "dysfunctional" and "codependent" are legitimate terms, but beware of using them as cop-outs because you aren't willing to really change your behavior or your habits.

Kevin Leman
Bringing Up Kids without Tearing Them Down

The people who influence us most are not those who buttonhole us and talk to us, but those who live their lives like the stars in heaven and the lilies in the field, perfectly simply and unaffectedly. Those are the lives that mold us.

Oswald Chambers
My Utmost for His Highest

f there is anything we wish to change in the child, we should first examine it and see whether it is not something that could be better changed in ourselves.

Carl G. Jung
psychologist

If [children] can't trust *your* promises, how will they learn to trust the promises of God?

Greg Johnson and Mike Yorkey

Faithful Parents, Faithful Kids

We must view young people not as empty bottles to be filled, but as candles to be lit.

Robert H. Shaffer

Parenthood is a partnership with God. You are not molding iron nor chiseling marble; you are working with the Creator of the universe in shaping human character and determining destiny.

Ruth Vaughn

Many [children] are drowning in the meaninglessness of a culture that rewards greed and guile and tells them that life is about getting rather than giving.

Marian Wright Edelman

The Measure of Our Success

Giving your kid a dollar for the church offering and five dollars for the movies not only demonstrates a parent's values, but is likely to produce the same value system in the child.

Unknown

In matters of style, swim with the current; in matters of principle, stand like a rock.

Thomas Jefferson

After nine years of public service and heading up three government offices, I have come to the conclusion that the issues surrounding the culture and our values are the most important ones.

William J. Bennett

The Devaluing of America

The quick response to moral breakdown is to appoint committees to make new codes to guide our ethics. But we do not fail because we lack codes. We fail because we lack character.

Lewis Smedes
A Pretty Good Person

God will not look you over for medals, degrees, or diplomas, but for scars.

Elbert Hubbard
as quoted in *A Man's Work Is Never Done*
by David Z. Nowell

To see things in the seed, that is genius.

Lao-tzu
as quoted in *Chicken Soup for the Soul*
by Jack Canfield and Mark Victor Hansen

f we want to teach honesty, then we must be prepared to listen to bitter truths as well as to pleasant truths. If a child is to grow up honest, he must not be encouraged to lie about his feelings. It is from our reaction to his expressed feelings that the child learns whether or not honesty is the best policy. When punished for truth, children lie in self-defense.

Dr. Haim G. Ginott

Between Parent and Child

It is only by thinking about great and good things that we come to love them, and it is only by loving them that we come to long for them; it is only by longing for them that we are impelled to seek after them; and it is only by seeking after them that they become ours.

Henry Van Dyke

W hat matters ultimately in the culture wars is what we do in our daily lives—not the big statements that we broadcast to the world at large, but the small messages we send through our families and our neighborhoods and our communities. . . . The future will depend not so much on the movers and shakers in the centers of power, but on the hopes that we generate in our own communities, our schools, our churches, synagogues, and families.

Michael Medved

as quoted in *The Devaluing of America*
edited by William J. Bennett

You don't raise heroes, you raise sons. And if you treat them like sons, they'll turn out to be heroes, even if it's just in your own eyes.

Walter M. Schirra Sr.

It's not just whether it's legal or illegal; it's whether it's right or wrong.

Ralph Giannola
VP Marriott Corporation
as quoted in *26 Business Virtues* by Seth Godin

Sometimes we're so concerned about giving our children what we never had growing up, we neglect to give them what we did have growing up.

Dr. James Dobson

t is easy to see that the moral sense has been bred out of certain sections of the population, like the wings have been bred off certain chickens to produce more white meat on them. This is a generation of wingless chickens.

Flannery O'Connor
as quoted in *Killing the Spirit* by Page Smith

The chains of habit are too small to be felt until they are too strong to be broken.

Benjamin R. Dejung
as quoted in *Killing Giants, Pulling Thorns*
by Charles Swindoll

All work, from the simplest chore to the most challenging and complex under-taking, is a wonder and a miracle. It is a gift and a blessing that God has given us. . . . To work is to do something essential to our humanness.

Ben Patterson

as quoted in *A Working Woman's Guide to Joy*
compiled by Gwen Weising

There is something very beautiful in work which is well and precisely done. It is a participation in the activity of God who makes all things well and wisely, beautiful to the last detail.

Jean Vanier
Community and Growth

Manual labor to my father was not only good and decent for its own sake, but, as he was given to saying, it straightened out one's thoughts, a contention which I have since proved on many occasions; indeed, the best antidote I know to a confused head or to tangled emotions is work with one's hands. To scrub a floor has alleviated many a broken heart and to wash and iron one's clothes brought order and clarity to many a perplexed and anxious mind.

Mary Ellen Chase

"A Goodly Fellowship," *A Man's Work Is Never Done*
by David Z. Nowell

Children very often are brought up
believing they are guests in the home
because they have nothing to do
except live there.

G. Bowden Hunt

as quoted in *The Gift of Family*
by Naomi Rhode

If God simply handed us everything we want, he'd be taking from us our greatest prize—the joy of accomplishment.

Frank A. Clark

as quoted in *A Working Woman's Guide to Joy*
compiled by Gwen Weising

Part
Three
Celebration

Home is the place of living and laughing. It is the place where I learn to play, to have fun, to relax. To live in celebration means there is an abundance of laughter at my house. Parties, presents, candles, Christmas trees, gifts, surprises, rocky road ice cream, jokes, games, backyard picnics, hilarity, thrills, vacations, field trips, hikes, bike rides, swimming, fishing, and sports—all are part of celebration.

Home is where I have my swing set, a tree house, a tent, sleeping bags, a basketball hoop, baseball gloves, skates, and a sandbox. Home is eating cold watermelon together on a hot day in the backyard and building a snowman six months later in the same place.

Home is where real living takes place. We work, play, eat, ride in cars together, attend basketball and soccer games and band concerts, watch videos, host overnight parties, develop our own private family jokes. In a home of celebration we do not take life too seriously but keep our senses of humor. In a home of celebration we relish hospitality and conversation. At home I learn that humor and laughter are good medicine.

When home is a place of celebration, all of this happens in a way that says, "This is what life is all about. There is no more and no less to the essence of meaning on this earth than this. Life, in a nutshell, is right here in this household. It is where I am celebrated!"

In short, home is where I discover wonder and learn to dream. I experience *our* traditions, *our* feasts, and *our* ceremonies. It is where I find joy.

want to be remembered
as someone who was fun
to live with.

Billy Graham

as quoted in *Go for the Magic*
by Pat Williams

Children learn from their parents whether life is a wonderful adventure or an endurance of one disappointment after another.

Valerie Bell

*Getting Out of Your Kids' Faces
and into Their Hearts*

None are so old as those who have outlived enthusiasm.

Henry David Thoreau

Celebration is central to all the Spiritual Disciplines. Without a joyful spirit of festivity the Disciplines become dull, death-breathing tools in the hands of modern Pharisees.

Richard Foster
Celebration of Discipline

think it is often just as sacred to laugh as it is to pray or preach or witness.

Charles Swindoll

Growing Strong in the Seasons of Life

God is a God of laughter, as well as of prayer . . . a God of singing, as well as of tears. God is at home in the play of His children. He loves to hear us laugh.

Peter Marshall

A well-developed sense of humor is the pole that adds balance to your steps as you walk the tightrope of life.

William A. Ward
as quoted in *The Gift of Family*
by Naomi Rhode

Let your eyes light up when your children are around. Laugh more. Tell them how empty and quiet it is when they're not there. Enjoy the things they bring to your life. Attend their activities, not as if they were compulsory for parents, but throw yourself into their lives.

Valerie Bell

Getting Out of Your Kids' Faces and into Their Hearts

One joy scatters a hundred griefs.

Chinese proverb

Sad are the children of parents who have no time for . . . "nonsense." (Unfortunately, many parents know that summer has arrived only because someone has turned on an air conditioner.) Such people are preoccupied with grubbing out a living, with making ends meet, and with watching sports spectaculars on television.

John Powell

Fully Human, Fully Alive

The life without festival is a long road without an inn.

Democritus of Abdera
as quoted in *Family Traditions That Last a Lifetime*
by Karen M. Ball and Karen L. Tornberg

During these family years—while your children are getting their emotional cues from you—learn to sing. If you love your babes, kick up your heels and learn to sing well! Let your laughter teach your children that all is well, that life is worth living, and worth living to the full.

Valerie Bell

*Getting Out of Your Kids' Faces
and into Their Hearts*

f we refuse to take time, we miss something
precious. A magical moment that may
happen only once in an entire lifetime . . .
is held in memory forever.

Charlotte Carpenter

In the Glass Meadow

f there is one thing I have learned from these

years, it is that it is not only okay but

actually good to take life as it comes.

Polly Berrien Berends

Gently Lead

First I was dying to finish high school and start college.

And then I was dying to finish college and start working.

And then I was dying to marry and have children.

And then I was dying for my children to grow old enough
for school so I could return to work.

And then I was dying to retire.

And now, I am dying . . . and suddenly I realize I forgot
to live.

Anonymous

as quoted in *What Every Mom Needs*
by Elisa Morgan and Carol Kuykendall

Gratitude is our gladness. We were born to it. Inside the itchy hankering to every heart stirs an aching need to feel grateful. We are heavy until we feel the lightness of gratitude. We hear the sweet music of joy only when we feel some awe and wonder and delight, and surprise, too, at being our own best gift. But once we have felt it, we know that there is no pleasure on earth like it.

Lewis Smedes

A Pretty Good Person

He who has little and says it is enough has more than he who has much and wants more.

Unknown

Life is easier if you dread only one day at a time.

Charles M. Schulz

as quoted in *Go for the Magic*
by Pat Williams

Yesterday is history.

Tomorrow is a mystery.

Today is a gift.

That's why we call it "The Present."

Anonymous

as quoted in *What Every Mom Needs*
by Elisa Morgan and Carol Kuykendall

A good laugh is sunshine
in a house.

William Makepeace Thackeray

f all must be right with the world before I may have a fling with joy, I shall be somber forever. . . . Joy in a world that does not work right must be a generous joy. Joy is always, always in spite of the fact that the whole world is groaning while it waits for its redemption.

Lewis Smedes

Shame and Grace

Work is fine, but when it's mixed with fun it's a lot better. Don't be a fun pauper. Get into the delights a good God has put into the world.

Norman Vincent Peale

When there are children in our life, it's always dancing season—even if we must occasionally dance with a limp!

Valerie Bell

*Getting Out of Your Kids' Faces
and into Their Hearts*

We ought to treat fun reverently. It is a mystery. It cannot be caught like a virus. It cannot be trapped like an animal. When it does come in, on little dancing feet, you probably won't be expecting it. In fact, I bet it comes when you're doing your duty or your work. It may even come on a Tuesday.

Suzanne Britt Jordan

New York Times reporter

Each second we live is a new and unique moment of the universe, a moment that will never be again. . . . And what do we teach our children? We teach them that two and two make four, and that Paris is the capital of France.

When will we also teach them what they are? We should say to each of them: Do you know what you are? You are a marvel. You are unique. In all the years that have passed, there has never been another child like you. Your legs, your arms, your clever fingers, and the way you move.

Pablo Casals
as quoted in *Chicken Soup for the Soul*
by Jack Canfield and Mark Victor Hansen

Times have changed, and we can probably count on their continuing to change. So it's up to us to seek out the little pieces of life that will become our children's memories.

Sylvia Harney

Every Time I Go Home, I Break Out in Relatives

One grandfather we know makes the rounds to his grandchildren's homes every Saturday morning to drop off doughnuts. Traditions are too significant as underpinnings to save only for major occasions.

Mimi Wilson and Mary Beth Lagerborg

Table Talk

Playing with our children is important enough to deserve priority in our lives. It's a lot more important—and more fun—than reading every word of the newspaper or cleaning out a closet.

**Linda Albert and
Michael Popkin**

Quality Parenting

Traditions identify us like a fingerprint. They anchor us. If we did not have these particular traditions, we would have others. That is because traditions insist upon themselves: Look around, and you will see them trying to exist everywhere, in everyone's life. Clearly we need them.

Elizabeth Berg
Family Traditions

If a child is to keep alive his inborn sense of wonder, he needs the companionship of at least one adult who can share it, rediscovering with him the joy, excitement, and mystery of the world we live in.

Rachel Carson
The Sense of Wonder

Why are the thoughts of children so delightful to us grown-ups? I think it's because of the vast gulf between their world and ours. Where we adults see the tired old commonplace of everyday life, these "babes" see a freshness, a wonderland waiting to be explored. They are wiser than we, in a way . . . because we have forgotten the magic of things, the wonder all around us.

Art Linkletter
Kids Say the Darndest Things!

Give the dreamers room. Go easy on the "shouldn'ts" and "can'ts," OK? Dreams are fragile things that have a hard time emerging in a cloud of negativism.

Charles Swindoll

The Quest for Character

've been thinking about seeing. There are lots of things to see, unwrapped gifts and free surprises. The world is fairly studded and strewn with pennies cast broadside from a generous hand.

Annie Dillard
Pilgrim at Tinker Creek

Part
Four
Boundaries

Home gives life form and context. It is a place that teaches me the rules for living. Home helps me "feel the envelope," and in that sense it gives me security, a sense of definition, and a sense of order. At home I learn the meaning of the word *authority*.

Home will not give me everything I want. It will balance earned responsibility and accountability with my freedoms. Home will build a scaffold, with the understanding that the eventual goal is to let the building stand on its own.

Home is like the stick that supports the young willow tree. It is there for a vital purpose, but its function fades with age.

Home is a place that eventually lets me go. Like a young eagle, I am allowed to fly to new heights. Home will not stifle me or force me to stay in the nest. It will slowly give me my freedom—freedom to try and fail, freedom to sin and be forgiven, freedom to make choices. Home will allow me to grow up.

Home is where parents understand that kids are on loan from God, to shape and nurture for flight. In this sense, their parenting role is not a lifelong responsibility; it lasts for only a season.

At home I am held, confined, defined, shaped, molded, fueled—and then launched!

When correcting a child, the goal is to apply light, not heat.

attributed to
Woodrow Wilson

Discipline is demanded of the athlete to win a game. Discipline is required for the captain running his ship. Discipline is needed for the pianist to practice for the concert. . . . If parents believe standards are necessary, then discipline certainly is needed to attain them.

Gladys Brooks
as quoted in *The Gift of Family*
by Naomi Rhode

Disciplining your child tells him that you are concerned about his behavior and you care about how he acts; in other words, you love him. Most children will tell you that when grown-ups let you do anything you want, it's scary. And if they could articulate their feelings, they would say, "My parents don't care what I do, and that means they don't love me."

Dr. Lee Salk

Familyhood

The goal of parental discipline should be the achievement of the child's self-discipline, not parental control of the child's behavior.

Janice Presser

Inspiring Parenthood

Pay attention to the intensity of your criticism. No matter how concrete your message, if you rebuke a child in fury, the child is more likely to focus on your emotion than on what you say.

Kathleen Cushman

"Why Shame Hurts So Much," *Parents* magazine

praise loudly. I blame softly.

Catherine the Great

as quoted in *A Man's Work Is Never Done*
by David Z. Nowell

Your parenting style always boils down to how you used your authority over your children.

Kevin Leman

Bringing Up Kids without Tearing Them Down

We should not use anger so often that it becomes an expected emotion. All of us, including our kids, love emotion. Once kids get used to a particular emotion— be it shame, anger, guilt, or love—that expected emotion becomes the emotion of choice.

Foster Cline and Jim Fay

Parenting with Love and Logic

iscipline is an external boundary, designed to develop internal boundaries in our children. It provides a structure of safety until the child has enough structure in his character to not need it. Good discipline always moves the child toward more internal structure and more responsibility.

Henry Cloud and John Townsend

Boundaries

The idea [of having boundaries] is not to insulate children but to equip them— not with our fragile cocoon but with the whole armor of God.

David Veerman

Parenting Passages

Parents need to learn the difference between holding a hand and chaining a soul.

Unknown

Watch your face and tone of voice when you criticize a child. Involuntary facial expressions of disdain or disgust carry powerful messages that the child is unworthy of acceptance and love.

Kathleen Cushman
"Why Shame Hurts So Much," *Parents* magazine

When we deal with our children, we must remember that they are children.

Zig Ziglar
Raising Positive Kids in a Negative World

t is critical that the parents
be parents and the children
be children.

**Frank and
Mary Alice Minirth**
Passages of Marriage

Discipline is like the stick a tree farmer ties to a young seedling: It is a guide to growing straight that is held firm to the very small sprout and is loosened as the fledgling tree grows.

Janice Presser

Inspiring Parenthood

hildren love their parents, but they cannot handle being equal with them. Deep down they do not see themselves as grown up. . . . Teens know they need guidance and leadership. Parents, it's up to us to give it to them.

Patsy Lovell
"Hold Fast," *Focus on the Family* magazine

A limit must be stated in a manner that is deliberately calculated to minimize resentment and to save self-esteem. The very process of limit setting should convey authority, not insult.

Dr. Haim G. Ginott
Between Parent and Child

Where do kids go when the empathic envelope is too tight or too loose? To that other readily available envelope— the peer group.

Dr. Ron Taffel

Parenting by Heart

T rain" is a word of deep importance for every parent to understand. Training is not telling, not teaching, not commanding, but something higher than all of these. It is not only telling a child what to do, but showing him how to do it and seeing that it is done.

Andrew Murray
How to Raise Your Children for Christ

Rules belong to life the way the scale belongs to music. And the way grammar belongs to writing. We cannot live the moral life without rules any more than we can make music without scales. Or write a story without grammar.

Lewis Smedes

Choices

ow we approach boundaries and child rearing will have enormous impact on the characters of our kids. On how they develop values. On how well they do in school. On the friends they pick. On whom they marry. And on how well they do in a career.

Henry Cloud and John Townsend

Boundaries

Good parents give their children roots and wings. Roots to know where home is, wings to fly away and exercise what's been taught them.

**Jonas Salk as told to
Bettie B. Youngs**
as quoted in *Chicken Soup for the Soul*
by Jack Canfield and Mark Victor Hansen

And now you wear a cap and gown. As the tassel shifts, so do all of our lives, to make a way for a solo stanza in the song of your existence. Yet we always sing the choruses together—around campfires, on beaches, in tour busses, at bedtime, in summer, at the breakfast table, after late-night dates. And the song is "joy."

Gloria Gaither
in a letter to her daughter
We Have This Moment

Hold everything in your hands lightly—otherwise it hurts when God pries your fingers open.

Corrie ten Boom
as quoted in *The Gift of Family*
by Naomi Rhodes

A child needs both to be hugged and unhugged. The hug lets her know she is valuable. The unhug lets her know that she is viable. If you're always shoving your children away, they will cling to you for love. If you're always holding them close, they will cling to you for fear.

Polly Berrien Berends
Gently Lead

Part Five
Refuge

Home is a place of refuge. It is a place of peace, a place that accepts me and binds my wounds. It has familiar sights and smells. At home I can let down my guard, set aside my assumed roles, do away with pretenses, and be myself.

Home is a place of harmony. It is like a sanctuary from the noise of life. I can hide there if I choose.

At home I have loving people to lean on, to lift me, to rejuvenate my spirit, to cuddle me. Home gives me permission to be vulnerable. It is a place of encouragement. It is a place with grace. At home I find forgiveness.

Home is a place of order and simplicity. I find familiar things there. It gives me my own space, my room, my pictures, my bed, my clothes and closet, my books and journals, my family.

Home is where families mend each other. We are each a part of the fabric of those we love. When home is a refuge, this is where we do daily repairs for hurts, apprehensions, and wounds inflicted on those we love.

In this place, I am welcome. I am safe.

When a first-grade pupil was asked what he had learned the first day in school, he said: "First of all, I learned that my name isn't Precious—it's Henry."

Unknown

We are born helpless. As soon as we are fully conscious, we discover loneliness. We need others physically, emotionally, intellectually; we need them if we are to know anything, even ourselves.

C. S. Lewis

Long years you've kept the door ajar
To greet me, coming from afar.
Long years in my accustomed place
I've read my welcome in your face.

Robert Bridges

have learned that I am a caretaker, not a custodian.

John Gillies
as quoted in *The Making of a Marriage*

A baby is God's opinion that the world should go on.

Carl Sandburg

Home is the place where, when you go there, they have to take you in.

Robert Frost
"The Death of the Hired Man"

The parent [is] audience. . . . In this role we applaud our children into existence, stroke them with our eyes toward greater feats of daring that might otherwise go undone. "Watch me!" commands the five-year-old, clinging with a death grip to the edge of the swimming pool. And we do watch him as the hypotenuse between one angle of the pool and the other is negotiated. We have borne him across the deep with our eyes.

Phyllis Theroux

Night Lights

Different does not mean
"wrong," it does not mean
"bad," it just means "different."

**Jerry D. Hardin and
Dianne C. Sloan**

Getting Ready for Marriage Workbook

Although there are many trial marriages, there is no such thing as a trial child.

Gail Sheehy
author of *Passages*

One day your children should be able to look back and say, "My family was the one place where I felt I could be myself—and be loved for it."

Bill Hybels
"Eight Traits of a Healthy Family,"
Today's Christian Woman magazine

But we were as gentle among you as a mother feeding and caring for her own children.

THE BIBLE
1 Thessalonians 2:7

The place where you live is the place where you will have the most opportunities to serve the Lord by serving others.

Mother Teresa

It is better to bind your children
to you by a feeling of respect,
and by gentleness, than by fear.

Terence

race and peace are twin sisters, grace
being the firstborn. Where grace abounds,
peace thrives. Where grace is stunted,
peace shrivels.

Charles F. Stanley

A Touch of His Peace

If you judge people, you have no time to love them.

Mother Teresa

Forgiveness is a divine
absurdity. For-give-ness is
a holy, complete, unqualified
giving.

Walter Wangerin Jr.

As for Me and My House

God is spreading grace around in the world like a five-year-old spreads peanut butter: thickly, sloppily, eagerly, and if we are in the back shed trying to stay clean, we won't even get a taste.

Donna Schaper
Stripping Down

The most important thing a
father can do for his children
is to love their mother.

Theodore Hesburg
as quoted in *Family Love* by Alfred H. Ells

Kindness is contagious. The spirit of harmony trickles down by a thousand secret channels into the inmost recesses of the household life.

Henry Van Dyke

A happy marriage is the union of two good forgivers.

Robert Quillen

as quoted in *Family Traditions That Last a Lifetime*
by Karen M. Ball and Karen L. Tornberg

Peace comes from living a measured life. . . .
My relationships are not what I do when I
have time left over from my work. . . .
Reading is not something I do when life
calms down. Prayer is not something I do
when I feel like it. They are all channels of
hope and growth for me. They must all be
given their due.

Joan D. Chittister
Wisdom Distilled from the Daily

Whe I get home from a long day or hard day I like to run through my home and make sure things are the same as when I left. The power of home is beyond imagining.

Matthew Merner, age nine
as quoted in *Where the Heart Is: Reflections on the Meaning of Home*

n a home that's a refuge, chores can wait a
few moments while a child strokes and
confides in a cat. A father can watch
television with a bowl of popcorn in his
lap and choose not to answer the phone.
A mother can relax in the tub undisturbed
while her worries melt away.

**Mimi Wilson and
Mary Beth Lagerborg**

Table Talk

Those who fear the Lord are
secure; he will be a place
of refuge for their children.

THE BIBLE
Proverbs 14:26

If we have no privacy, we have no sacredness:
We lose our boundaries, and we have no
place within that is holy to ourselves. Take
away our sacredness, and we lose our core.

Lewis Smedes

Shame and Grace

Respect the child. Be not too much his parent. Trespass not on his solitude.

Ralph Waldo Emerson

We need to find God, and he cannot be found in noise and restlessness. God is the friend of silence.

Mother Teresa

ome to me is not just a roof over my head, but a dream. If I lost my home it would be like losing all my thoughts, dreams, and memories. I love everything about it, from the north of the house to the south of the house. From the east of the house to the west of the house. If a fire burned down my house, the tears would roll down my face like the water down dirty windows.

Allison Slater, age nine
as quoted in *Where the Heart Is: Reflections on the Meaning of Home*

After twenty years of wear, the worn places on the seats and scuff marks on the rungs speak of use and of life. The table, marred by model glue and a pumpkin carving knife, is haunted with memories of a host of friends and of our children from high chairs to high school. It represents the best of what we've had and of what we will have together as a family and as a team.

**Mimi Wilson and
Mary Beth Lagerborg**

Table Talk

Part Six
Connection

The family is my first and most important bond. Home offers my first experience of true intimacy. I am connected through love—unconditional, affirming love. I am hugged and touched, fawned over, adored.

At home I am listened to, heard, and understood. My family notices me, the small changes in me. And even though I sometimes do not want to talk about those changes, it is comforting to know they notice. At home someone shows keen interest in my life, my trials and triumphs. I learn about tough love that will not let me run roughshod over myself or others.

As a family we do things together. We eat together. We do chores together. We take vacations together. We ride in cars together. We attend concerts, ball games, and church together.

At home I learn what it means to keep commitments and vows. It is a prelude to a marriage bond, and its quality has everything to do with the quality of that future bond.

In short, I am attached to—forever connected with—a group of people whom I did not choose. This is my family, unique with all of its quirks—but it is *mine*. It is my link, my genealogy. And without it I would not exist. I cherish it almost more than life itself.

Two people can accomplish more than twice as much as one. . . . If one person falls, the other can reach out and help. . . . A person standing alone can be attacked and defeated, but two can stand back-to-back and conquer. Three are even better, for a triple-braided cord is not easily broken.

THE BIBLE
Ecclesiastes 4:9-10, 12

Once I sat under a mulberry tree with some bigger kids and tried to smoke some cigarette butts that they had picked up along the curb, but I became awfully dizzy and I sneaked home sick. It was a Tuesday, so my mother was there to take me in, which she did, and when she smelled what I had been up to, she said that any boy who got that sick from smoking needed an ice-cream cone to calm his stomach. She gave my older brother a nickel and shooed him off to the drugstore to buy me one.

Lewis Smedes

Shame and Grace

When we're available to our children it says, "You are important." And when we're not available it says, "Oh, yes, I love you, but other things still come ahead of you. You are not really that important."

Josh McDowell

How to Be a Hero to Your Kids

No one who reaches the end of life has ever looked back and said, "Oh, I wish I had spent more time at the office instead of with my kids."

Greg Johnson and Mike Yorkey

Daddy's Home

We make a living by what
we get, but we make a life
by what we give.

Winston Churchill

Quality moments with your children come out of spending as much time with them as you can.

Kevin Leman
Bringing Up Kids without Tearing Them Down

A large majority [of Americans] claim that family is the most important thing in life, but surveys show that most people will put their jobs, possessions, and personal freedom before family responsibilities. . . . If you watch what Americans do, traditional family relationships are in trouble.

American Demographics

Money, status, career, power, and a thousand other pursuits may burn brightly for a time in our lives. But when winds of reflection clear away the smoke, nothing satisfies or fulfills a man more profoundly than the genuine love and praise of his children.

Paul Lewis

as quoted in *Family Traditions That Last a Lifetime*
by Karen M. Ball and Karen L. Tornberg

Functional parents are loving, firm but fair, consistent, affectionate, forgiving, sacrificial, encouraging, wise, humble, and strong. They also have date books or month-at-a-glance calendars with plenty of dates with their children already scheduled.

Kevin Leman
Bringing Up Kids without Tearing Them Down

Communication implies sound.
Communion doesn't.

Madeleine L'Engle

Children of all ages need meaningful touch, particularly from a father. Studies show that mothers touch their children in more nurturing ways, and fathers in more playful ways. But when the children were interviewed, perhaps because it didn't happen as often, they perceived their father's touch as more nurturing.

Robert Salt

as quoted in *The Gift of the Blessing*
by Gary Smalley and John Trent

The truth is that from the day we're born until the day we die we need to feel held and contained somewhere. We can let go and become independent only when we feel sufficiently connected to other people.

Dr. Ron Taffel

Parenting by Heart

took off my uniform and started for the showers, and standing over at the far wall was my dad. He had been there for 2½ hours and he had not come into my cubicle. We locked eyes. He stood up straight and said to me, "Hey, great game!" I burst into tears. Compliments from my dad never had been easy coming, and I reached out and we hugged each other. From that moment, I knew my dad.

Mark Harmon
NFL quarterback
as quoted in *Things I Should Have Said to My Father*
compiled by Joanna Powell

Our most basic instinct is not for survival, but for family. Most of us would give our own life for the survival of a family member. . . . Such a group is the basic building block of our world, the place where the miracle of "us" takes place.

Paul Pearsall
The Power of the Family

Listening is loving.

Zig Ziglar

Courtship after Marriage

t is impossible to overemphasize the immense need
humans have to be really listened to, to be taken seriously,
to be understood. No one can develop freely in this world
and find a full life without feeling understood by at least
one person. . . . Listen to all the conversations of our
world, between nations as well as those between couples.
They are for the most part dialogues of the deaf.

Paul Tournier
To Understand Each Other

n the all-important world of family
relations, three words are almost as
powerful as the famous "I love you."
They are, "Maybe you're right."

Oren Arnold

as quoted in *Family Traditions That Last a Lifetime*
by Karen M. Ball and Karen L. Tornberg

Listening . . . means taking a vigorous, human interest in what is being told us. You can listen like a blank wall or like a splendid auditorium where every sound comes back fuller and richer.

Alice Duer Miller

Promises from Parents

ost people do not really listen with the intent to under-stand; rather, they listen with the intent to reply.

Stephen Covey
as quoted in *Family Love* by Alfred H. Ells

Our work on this earth is simply to love the Father with our whole heart, to show His love to others, and to learn to listen for His voice in all that happens in our lives. To listen for that voice in the confident, curious wisdom of the little ones among us, in the memories and stories of our lives, and, yes, even in the death of the ones we love.

**Gloria Gaither and
Shirley Dobson**

Let's Hide the Word

Communication is give and take. Preaching is give.

**Frank Minirth,
Brian Newman,
and Paul Warren**

The Father Book

Do you know what I am?" a teenager once asked. "I'm a comma."

"What do you mean?" the listener replied.

"Well, whenever I talk to my dad, he stops talking and makes a 'comma.' But when I'm finished, he starts right up again as if I hadn't said a thing. I'm just a comma in the middle of his speeches."

Unknown
as quoted in *Why Wait?*
by Josh McDowell and Dick Day

Children need more than food, shelter, and clothing. The bottom line is: Every child needs at least one person who's crazy about him.

Fran Stott

dean of the Erickson Institute for
Advanced Study in Child Development

emember this: Love is not a state of being. It's an act of the will. It cannot be demanded or required or commanded. It can only be bestowed.

Jerry Jenkins

Twelve Things I Want My Kids to Remember Forever

To love and be loved is to feel the sun from both sides.

David Viscott

We cannot make the Kingdom of God happen, but we can put out leaves as it draws near. We can be kind to each other. We can be kind to ourselves. We can drive back the darkness a little. We can make green places within ourselves and among ourselves where God can make his Kingdom happen.

Frederick Buechner

The Clown in the Belfry

little criticism makes me angry, and a little rejection makes me depressed. A little praise raises my spirits, and a little success excites me. It takes very little to raise me up or thrust me down.

Henri Nouwen
The Return of the Prodigal Son

Hugging is healthy. It helps the body's immune system, it keeps you healthier, it cures depression, it reduces stress, it induces sleep, it's invigorating, it's rejuvenating, it has no unpleasant side effects, and hugging is nothing less than a miracle drug.

Unknown
as quoted in *Chicken Soup for the Soul*
by Jack Canfield and Mark Victor Hansen

Some luck lies in not getting what you thought you wanted but getting what you have, which once you have it you may be smart enough to see is what you would have wanted had you known.

Garrison Keillor
Lake Wobegon Days

Perhaps the most profound effect of television watching . . . is its effect on family relationships. Regular television viewing deprives families of opportunities to interact with one another.

William Kilpatrick

Why Johnny Can't Tell Right from Wrong

Y ou know, once when I heard an interviewer ask George [Bush] what accomplishment he was most proud of, I wondered what would he answer? Would he say his years as a Navy pilot, a businessman, a public servant, or would he speak about some of the changes that happened since he has been president? . . . What would he answer? Well, it's the same answer George Bush always gives—that his children still come home.

Barbara Bush

as quoted in *Family Traditions That Last a Lifetime*
by Karen M. Ball and Karen L. Tornberg

In the end, memories have much more power than decor.

Baroness Raffaello de Banfield
as quoted in *Architectural Digest*

Ordinary people are messengers of the Most High. They go about their tasks in holy anonymity. Often, even unknown to themselves. Yet, if they had not been there, if they had not said what they said or did what they did, it would not be the way it is now. . . . Never forget that you too might be a messenger.

Lawrence Kushner
"Honey from the Rock," *100 Ways to Keep Your Soul Alive*
by Frederic and Mary Ann Brussat

Part
Seven
Legacy

Home is a place with a history to pass on to me. Home gives me a foundation, a past that lends my existence a place, a sense of belonging, a historical context. Home is where stories get passed on for generations.

Home is where my photo is taken every so often, not only to prove I grew up, but to document my house, my backyard, my friends, my school. It shows how we celebrated holidays, birthdays, family, and best friends.

Home gives me a legacy: a racial and ethnic background I can understand and embrace, a family tree to which I can relate and be attached, a faith to which I can return.

Home is where I am told that when I smile a certain way, I remind my mom of my grandpa Floyd; that my name, William, means "conqueror" and has been passed on for four generations. Home is where I hear the stories of my birth, my parents' courtship, and my antics with my siblings. I hear the stories of my country through the filter of my own genealogy. Wars, depressions, family migrations, as well as ancestral achievements and failures are taught to me through the history of my family.

Home is where I build my own legacy: the stories I was told I pass on to my children, adding my generation's story to the saga.

In short, I learn the legacy that makes us, "us," and me, "me." It is my identity. It is my roots. It is me.

One generation plants the
trees, the next sits in the shade.

Unknown

On a rainy Saturday afternoon, friends and relatives gathered in a small chapel to watch as my children, smiling and excited, stepped into the waters. We listened as Uncle Tom led each in their confession of faith: "Neil, tell us when Jesus Christ became your Lord." "Taylor, what does baptism mean?" "Jana, how will you keep on growing in Christ?" We applauded as each child came up—wet, pink and shining, like newborns. Then we sang "Great Is Thy Faithfulness," and Grandma Kopp closed with a prayer to the One who had opened their hearts. At that moment, it seemed to me our family was passing on the real inheritance.

David Kopp
Christian Parenting Today magazine

Do not resist growing old—
many are denied the privilege.

Unknown

Life is no brief candle to me. It is a sort of splendid torch which I have got hold of for the moment, and I want to make it burn as brightly as possible before handing it on to future generations.

George Bernard Shaw

What is to give light must endure burning.

Viktor Frankl

In all the conversations a parent has with one's children it seems increasingly important to me to give children our assurance that we have endured their same confusions and emerged to feel the sun on our backs. I suppose, to be uncomplicated about it, I want to give my children the gift of hope.

Phyllis Theroux
Night Lights

Tradition is that sense of continuity, whole-ness, immovability, changelessness, and stability, that single thread which unites and which brings comfort in lives bombarded by unceasing, unpredictable change. The world is moving fast, and we need a sense of belonging, a center, a history, and a future we can depend on.

Naomi Rhode

The Gift of Family

ou are not only making memories . . . you are the memories. In a deep subconscious, unarticulated place a parent stays with his or her child . . . forever!

Valerie Bell

Getting Out of Your Kids' Faces
and into Their Hearts

There are places we all come from—deep-rooty-common places—that make us who we are. And we disdain them or treat them lightly at our peril. We turn our backs on them at the risk of self-contempt. There is a sense in which we need to go home again—and can go home again. Not to recover home, no. But to sanctify memory.

Robert Fulghum

All I Really Need to Know I Learned in Kindergarten

Even though I was only twelve, I knew that in our family "remembering who you are" meant we were children of wonderful people with great ancestors of deep spiritual faith.

Naomi Rhode
The Gift of Family

It has been said that to understand someone,
you must know his or her memories.
To understand yourself, you need not only
anticipate a future, you must also remember
a past. What we yet will be is connected
to what we have already been. But that
connection is often a subtle, elusive one,
hard to grasp in the present moment.

Thomas R. Swears
"The Story-Shaped Life," *Weavings*

Children are a heritage
of the Lord.

THE BIBLE
Psalm 127:3, NKJV

know that you sincerely trust the Lord, for you have the faith of your mother, Eunice, and your grandmother, Lois.

THE BIBLE
2 Timothy 1:5

A family history is like a novel in progress with a full cast of characters and, because each of them is a part of you, you want to know them all.

Frederick Waterman
"November's Letters," *Hemispheres* magazine

Grandchildren are the crowning glory of the aged.

THE BIBLE
Proverbs 17:6

Consider history as inspiration—your family's, your country's, your religion's. I find history often beautiful and always interesting and helpful in providing perspective. It has a way of marking our place in the larger sense. It can give us a feeling like we get when we lie on our backs looking at the stars.

Elizabeth Berg
Family Traditions

We inherit from our ancestors gifts so often taken for granted. . . . We are links between the ages, containing past and present expectations, sacred memories and future promise. Only when we recognize that we are heirs can we truly be pioneers.

Edward C. Sellner

Mentoring

Years ago—probably centuries ago— some woman with nothing better to do determined that food should be passed in one direction only around the table. She decided which direction that was, and families have been disagreeing about it ever since.

Sylvia Harney

Every Time I Go Home, I Break Out in Relatives

The real histories of families aren't the records of births, deaths, and marriages. They are the stories told after dessert, when the coffee's been served and everyone's too full to move.

Frederick Waterman
"November's Letters," *Hemispheres* magazine

You, like every human being, are a storyteller by birthright. You are born with an endless supply of personal and universal themes.

Nancy Mellon
Storytelling and the Art of Imagination

We each have our own stories filled with rumors of angels. Elie Wiesel writes, "God made man because he loves stories." Discovering those personal stories is the essential expression of our spiritual quest. Without such stories we cannot be fully human, for without them we are unable to articulate or even understand our deepest experiences.

Sue Monk Kidd
"The Story-Shaped Life," *Weavings*

Anyone who tells a story
speaks a world into being.

Michael E. Williams
"Voices from Unseen Rooms:
Storytelling and Community," *Weavings*

read because my father read to me. And because he'd read to me, when my time came I knew intuitively there is a torch that is supposed to be passed from one generation to the next. And through countless nights of reading, I began to realize that when enough of the torchbearers—parents and teachers—stop passing the torches, a culture begins to die.

Jim Trelease

The Read Aloud Handbook

Storytelling . . . is a continual process of transforming sojourners into kinfolk and strangers into friends.

Michael E. Williams
"Voices from Unseen Rooms:
Storytelling and Community," *Weavings*

Tell it to your children,

and let your children tell it to

their children,

and their children to the next

generation.

THE BIBLE
Joel 1:3, NIV

t is time to rediscover that God created our lives story-shaped and to give serious attention to the scripting of our spiritual experience. Until we undertake the important work of discovering and shaping the inner tale, the interior life will remain a brooding chaos in need of an artist, a storyteller who can order it into a cosmos of meaning.

Sue Monk Kidd
"The Story-Shaped Life," *Weavings*